QUILTS ON SAFARI

Another title for this book could be An African Adventure into Quilting. Using traditional techniques, two sisters Jenny Williamson and Pat Parker, together with a group of quilters from southern Africa, have managed to capture the vibrancy and taste of Africa in the wonderful quilts shown throughout this book.

The colours and designs illustrated are pure ethnic Africa. Even the quilt titles conjures up images of the "dark and exotic" continent, *Scatterings of Africa, Sunburst, I Kyalami (My Home), Escapes, Tree of Life, Waterhole in the Moonlight, Starlight over Africa, African Autumn.* These are but some of the 30 plus quilts shown throughout the book, all of which are in full colour, often with a colour picture illustrating the inspiration from which the quilt originated.

The book contains complete instructions for 10 quilts and an African doll, Thandi. These instructions are suitable for the inexperienced to the expert quilter. But more than just telling the reader "How to" the book demonstrates colour and design techniques which will excite and stimulate the reader into simple and effective ideas from which they themselves, can create their own African images.

This book will delight any quilter who has a yearning to flavour Africa and create their own ethnic quilt.

FRONT AND BACK COVER: A variation of the quilt "African Autumn"

TITLE PAGE: An enlargement of the quilt "Scatterings of Africa"

First published 1998.

Published by:
Triple T Publishing c.c.
29 Colenso Road
Claremont 7700
Cape Town South Africa.

North American Distributor:
Quilters Resources Inc.
P.O. Box 148850
Chicago IL 60614
U.S.A.

Photographs: Rob Williamson
Reproduction: Full Colour Graphics Johannesburg
Printed by: Mills Litho Cape Town

COPYRIGHT© JENNY WILLIAMSON AND PAT PARKER: 1998

ISBN 0-958 3873-9-7

OTHER BOOKS PUBLISHED BY TRIPLE T PUBLISHING C.C.

SATIN AND SILK RIBBON EMBROIDERY
By Lesley Turpin Delport
ISBN 0-620 1775-5-1

JUST FLOWERS
By Lesley Turpin Delport
ISBN 0-958 3873-1-1

JUST DESIGNS
By Lesley Turpin Delport
ISBN 0-958 3873-7-0

THE CUSHIONS AND A QUILT
By Sue Akerman
ISBN 0-9583873-1-1

THE LIBERATED CANVAS
By Penny Cornell
ISBN 0-9583873-4-6

LET'S SMOCK IT
By Patricia Muñoz Timmins
ISBN 0-958 3873-8-9

CONTENTS

THE AUTHORS

It is said that one's characteristics, talents, intelligence, sporting prowess, etc. are to a large extent due to the genes inherited from one's parents, and if this is so, then surely our great love for needlework has been inherited from our mother, grandmother and great-grandmother before us.

We were born and grew up in Johannesburg, being third generation South Africans. Our great-grandmother, Elizabeth Davidson, travelled from Scotland to marry John Cruikshank, a trader and hunter, who was stationed in what was then known as Bechuanaland - now Botswana. Due to the many hardships of living in remote areas of Africa, Elizabeth had, of necessity, to make clothes and do the mending for her family, which consisted of three daughters. Her daughter, Jeannie, our grandmother, married Frederick Bristol, who had emigrated from the USA to South Africa. Frederick was one of a class of three, who were the first graduates of the University of Nevada in 1891. He came to the Transvaal in 1895 and became manager of the Jupiter, Robinson Deep and Knights Gold Mines. Jeannie had spent many hours sewing beside her mother and became wellknown for the wonderful fancy dress costumes she made for the children, who

PAT PARKER   JENNY WILLIAMSON

frequently won prizes at the parties which were so popular during those times. This talent for handwork was in turn passed down to her daughter, Jean, our mother, who married Percy Barnes, a wellknown and much respected schoolmaster in Johannesburg. Jean made all her own and our clothes and was particularly good at hand embroidery.

Neither of us can remember a time in our lives when we were not surrounded by fabric and were not engaged in some form of handwork, be it dressmaking or embroidery. Therefore when South African women started doing patchwork during the 70's it seemed natural for us to become involved in the quilting process.

We started teaching in 1978 and over the years have taken every opportunity (and still do) to attend classes given by both South African and Overseas teachers. We conduct basic, intermediate and advanced courses in piecing, applique, quilting and embroidery. We have taught courses at the South African National Quilt Festivals in Bloemfontein (1989), Durban (1990), Port Elizabeth (1992), Cape Town (1994), Durban (1996) and Port Elizabeth (1998). We have also taught at International Congresses held in South Africa.

We dedicate this book to our husbands, John and Rob, whose unfailing love and support have allowed us to indulge our passion for quiltmaking.

WE WOULD LIKE TO EXPRESS OUR SINCERE THANKS TO:

Our parents, who encouraged all our endeavours - for their guidance, wisdom, love and laughter. Our children, who are our most "telling" critics and also our greatest fans. Our grandchildren, who give us good reason to continue quiltmaking until well into the next century! Rob Williamson, for the time and effort he devoted in doing all the photography for this book. Rob, again, for placing a multitude of office facilities at our disposal. John Parker, for his help and guidance while writing the text of this book. Michéle Davies, for her inspiration, and for forcing us to leave our quilting 'Comfort Zone'! Southern Stars, our quilt group, for their support and friendship (not to mention fabrics) over many years of quilting. Shelley Joubert, for changing our rough sketches into professional artwork. Sheila Forbes, for all the computer work relating to the text. Brett Eloff, for allowing us to print his wonderful photograph of our President, Nelson Mandela. Our pupils over many years, especially those who allowed us to borrow their quilts for the publication of "Quilts on Safari", namely: Gaye Bertram, Joy Cowen, Joan Innes, Geraldine Lonsdale, Pat Perry, Marie-Claire Storme, Libby Steel and Barbara Tucker.

INTRODUCTION

The various techniques, information, materials, patterns, books and periodicals we in South Africa use in making our quilts come almost exclusively from overseas. This background has been essential in order to enable us to learn the basic fundamentals of patchwork, but now that so many of our quilters have the basic knowledge and skills we feel it is time to make quilts with an African flavour.

We would like to think that quilters worldwide would be interested in seeing the quilts shown in our book and may themselves be inspired to make quilts utilising the influences of Africa.

We have a vast cultural and environmental diversity of sources from which to gain inspiration. Our scenery is spectacular and this opens up countless opportunities for creating landscape quilts or wallhangings. Our flora and fauna are unique and adaptations can be used with motifs chosen from these sources. Quilts can be made dealing with subjects that are specifically relevant to life in this country, celebrating the lives of our multi-cultural population, from whatever background, showing their lifestyles, either past or present.

On the following pages we shall give examples of quilts which we believe have an essence of Africa about them. We have given instructions for a number of these quilts, perhaps quilters will copy them exactly, or better still, use them as a starting point in creating their own 'African' quilts.

Hopefully this book will help quilters, whether they be beginners or advanced, whether they prefer hand or machine work, whether they prefer piecing or applique, to produce quilts with an African flavour, using a combination of ethnic fabrics, shapes and colours and - what is more - to have fun doing so!

We would be thrilled at any time in the future to receive colour slides of any quilts resulting from an idea or inspiration gained from reading this book.

PAT AND JENNY

LET'S GET STARTED

As so many wonderful books have already been written giving all the necessary details of the various techniques used in quilting, we see no purpose in repeating these details. We would, however, like to mention the following factors that should be taken into account when making a quilt or wallhanging.

CHOICE OF FABRICS

As far as the choice of fabrics is concerned, this is a golden opportunity to leave your 'Comfort Zone'.

Whether it be artwork or clothing, the people of Africa invariably choose an unpredictable variety of vibrant and seemingly clashing colours. Do not forget this when planning a quilt.

Audition the fabrics, choosing the ones which are most suitable for huts, trees, people, animals, birds, etc. Move the fabrics around until the result is successful.

Do not be too inhibited. The more the variety introduced, the more successful the end result.

Introduce some startling 'Uglies'

Don't choose fabrics that are too realistic - naivety looks great!

Hand-dyed fabrics are good - particularly for backgrounds.

We recommend 100 percent cotton fabric for hand applique. When doing machine applique, however, use whatever fabric gives the desired effect, whether it be cotton blends, satin, wool, silk, organza, netting, etc.

HAND APPLIQUE

Due to the fact that it is often difficult to remove various marking pens and pencils, we use a method by which we do not have to mark the fabric at all.

Use a fine ballpoint pen to trace the design onto iron-on vylene. We prefer to use a vylene that is thin and pliable, with bonding only on one side.

When tracing the design onto the vylene, always have the bonded side down.

Cut vylene along the marked lines. (No seam allowance). Position the vylene onto the fabric as desired. The grain of the fabric is not important.

Iron the vylene lightly onto the right side of the fabric, placing a plain white sheet of paper between the iron and the work. (Should you inadvertently iron onto the wrong side of the vylene, only the vylene and paper will have to be replaced, not the iron!).

Use a dry iron, no steam, but do not allow it to be too hot (e.g. wool setting or cooler, depending upon your iron), otherwise the bonding will melt and cause the vylene to adhere too firmly to the fabric. It is always advisable to test on a scrap before commencing.

After vylene has been ironed in place, cut a seam allowance of between $1/8$" (3mm) and $1/4$" (6mm).

Working on a flat surface, pin applique pieces to base. We find the tiny applique pins indispensable, as the long ones tend to get in the way. These can cause serious stab wounds! Prevent bloodstains at all cost!

We sew with either an Applique or Crewel (Embroidery) needle (Size 9), but we suggest that whatever needle is correct for you is acceptable. If you have 'young eyes' and dainty fingers, by all means use a 12!

The best applique thread is 100 percent cotton. Match the thread as closely as possible to the colour of the piece being applied. If the match is not perfect always go for a darker rather than a lighter thread.

Sew small blind hemming stitches about $1/8$" (3mm) apart. Pull thread firmly upwards towards you as you go.

Concave curves need to be clipped to release the tension.
Remove vylene as each piece is applied.

MACHINE APPLIQUE

As in hand applique use a fine ballpoint pen to trace the design onto the vylene.

When tracing the design onto the vylene always have the bonded side up, and when ironing the vylene onto the fabric always have the bonded side down. Iron this onto the wrong side of the fabric. Do not worry about the grain, rather iron the vylene onto the fabric to obtain the best effect. Use a dry iron, but do not allow it to be too hot. Place a sheet of clean white paper between the iron and the work.

Use a zigzag machine with a suitable foot (one which has no metal or plastic between the toes to block your view as you sew).

When doing machine applique fibre deposits build up very quickly around the bobbin area, so it is necessary to clean and oil your machine regularly. Make sure that the needle is sharp, as a blunt needle is the main cause of irregular stitching. (We like to use a 70/10 or 80/12 size needle).

For satin stitch your stitches should be close enough to form a solid line, but not be so close that they bunch up and jam the machine. (If you let go of the fabric when sewing, the feed dog should carry the fabric through without a problem). For a more contemporary look alter your stitch lengths and widths until you get the desired effect. Try using different threads; this is an area that can be such a lot of fun! You may even wish to leave raw edges and sew with a straight stitch.
Remember that applique is a means of stitching one fabric to another. How it is done is not important as long as the end result is successful. This is where one can be really creative!

Always put a sheet of magazine paper underneath your work when machining, i.e. between your work and the feed dog. This will act as a stabiliser and prevent the work from puckering. When stitching is complete remember to remove the paper from the back of the work!

Pull threads to back of work and cut off as you go. Birds' nests are for trees - not for the backs of quilts!

Remember, anyone can do applique work. It is a medium that can be both rewarding and stimulating.

PIECING

Whether you are doing hand or machine piecing, it is imperative to work accurately. We use a ¼" (6mm) seam allowance throughout. If your seams are not exactly ¼" (6mm) you will need to adjust our given measurements. We suggest that you sew 3 small squares together. Cut them 2½" x 2½" (64mm x 64mm). When they are stitched they should measure 6½" (168mm) from the left to the right hand edges. If they do not, adjust the seam accordingly.

When using the piecing templates always add ¼" (6mm) seam allowance.

The arrow on the templates indicates the direction of the grain of the fabric.

PRESSING

Pressing means literally what it says - press the iron gently onto the fabric. If you push too hard you will stretch the fabric.

Press the seams as you go.

Do not open the seams as it weakens them.

Wherever possible press the seams towards the darkest fabric.

Press seams away from where you wish to quilt.

SIGNING YOUR QUILTS

Personalise your quilt.

Always sign and date your quilt - either on the front or back. Include any other information that you feel is relevant, e.g. maybe the name of the person or the occasion for which the quilt has been made.

LEAP YEAR IN THE LOWVELD

59" x 74"   150cm x 188 cm

PAT PARKER AND JENNY WILLIAMSON

This quilt was our first attempt at making an 'African Baltimore'. We have provided the designs that we used for our quilt, but these can be changed to make your quilt more personalised. The choice of fabrics for this quilt is perhaps more important than the actual design. Use strong vibrant fabrics and we are sure that your quilt will be successful.

LEAP YEAR IN THE LOWVELD

59" x 74"   150cm x 188 cm

PAT PARKER AND JENNY WILLIAMSON

Before starting this quilt please refer to the notes on hand applique and choice of fabrics.

TECHNIQUES:
Hand appliqued, machine pieced and hand quilted.

BLOCK SIZE:
The completed blocks should measure 11" **(280mm)**.
Please enlarge the drawings of pages 66 - 68 to this size.

MATERIALS:

Background fabric.	3 yds	**(3m)**
Applique swags on border (main fabric)	1 yd	**(1m)**
Final border	½ yd	**(½m)**
A variety of brightly coloured fabrics suitable for the applique and sashing strips between blocks.		
Backing.	63" x 78"	**(160 cm x 200 cm)**
Batting.	63" x 78"	**(160 cm x 200 cm)**
Binding.	½ yd	**(½ m)**
Iron-on vylene.	1 yd	**(1 m)**
Applique and embroidery threads.		

METHOD:
Using your background fabric cut the following:

2 strips along the length 60½" x 6½" **(1 537 mm x 165 mm) (K)**
2 strips along the length 45½" x 6½" **(1 155 mm x 165 mm) (L)**
12 squares 11½" x 11½" **(292 mm x 292 mm) (A)**.
4 squares 6½" x 6½" **(165 mm x 165 mm) (M)**

Applique the 12 large squares (A), the 4 border strips (K) and (L) and the 4 corner squares (M).

Using a variety of fabrics, cut sashing strips as follows :
Cut 12 strips 11½" x 1½" **(292 mm x 38 mm) (B)**
Cut 12 strips 12½" x 1½" **(318 mm X 38 mm) (C)**
Cut 12 strips 12½" x 1½½" **(318 mm x 38 mm) (D)**
Cut 12 strips 13½" x 1½" **(343 mm x 38 mm) (E)**
Cut 12 strips 13½" x 1½" **(343 mm x 38 mm) (F)**
Cut 12 strips 14½" x 1½" **(368 mm X 38 mm) (G)**
Cut 12 strips 14½" x 1½" **(368 mm x 38 mm) (H)**
Cut 12 strips 15½" x 1½" **(394 mm x 38 mm) (J)**
Sew these strips to each block in alphabetical order. Join blocks in rows 3 across by 4 down. Add borders (K) to left and right hand sides of quilt. Join 2 squares (M) to top and bottom borders (L). Sew to top and bottom of quilt. Using final border fabric cut 2 strips 72½" x 1½" **(1 842 mm x 38 mm) (N)**. Sew to left and right hand sides of quilt. Cut 2 strips 59½" x 1½" **(1 511 mm x 38 mm) (O)**. Sew to top and bottom of quilt. Embellish your quilt with embroidery. Shadow quilt in rows on backgrounds approximately ¼" **(6mm)** apart.
Bind quilt.

Drawings: Pages 66, 67, 68
Templates: Pages 69, 70

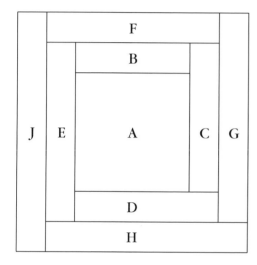

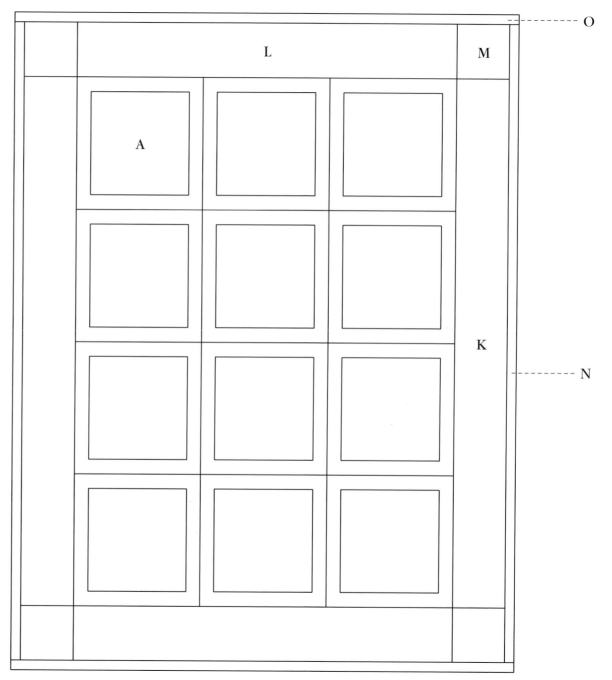

AFRICAN SUNBURST

47" X 65"   **120 cm x 165 cm**

GERALDINE LONSDALE

This is a Scrap Quilt and provides a golden opportunity to utilise all those 'Uglies' stashed away at the back of the cupboard. Mix them with your favourites and the result will be stunning. To achieve the wonderful stained-glass effect use as many bright vibrant fabrics as possible. Use all the reds, golds, oranges and yellows to represent the sun's rays.

AFRICAN SUNBURST

47" X 65"   120 cm x 165 cm

GERALDINE LONSDALE

Before starting this quilt please refer to the notes on piecing.

TECHNIQUE:
Hand pieced and hand quilted.

BLOCK SIZE:
8" x 8".(203 mm x 203 mm) You will need 24 blocks.

MATERIALS:
As many scraps as you can lay your hands on. Beg, borrow and steal from the quilters you know and those you don't !

Sashing strips and border	1½ yds (1½ m)
Sashing squares	¼ yd (¼ m)
Backing	51" x 69" (130 cm x 175 cm)
Batting	51" x 69" (130 cm x 175 cm)
Binding	½ yd (½ m)

METHOD:
Make templates.
Mark your fabric, then add the ¼" (6mm) seam allowance. Your piecing will be more accurate this way. Please note that templates marked "r" must be cut in reverse.
Referring to the block drawing make 24 blocks as follows :

Step 1   Sew (A) to (B)
Step 2   Sew (C) to (Cr)
Step 3   Join together (D) (E) (F) (E) (F) (E) (F) (E) (Dr).
Step 4   Join along all curves to form block.
Cut 58 sashing strips 8½" x 1½" (216 mm x 38 mm)
Cut 39 sashing squares 1½" x 1½" (38mm x 38 mm)

Lay out your blocks 4 across by 6 down. Working with the top 4 blocks add a sashing strip to the left hand side of each block and another strip to the right hand edge. Do the same with the remaining 5 rows.

Sew 5 sashing squares to 4 sashing strips, alternating the squares and strips to form a row.
Make another 6 rows.

Now sew these 13 rows together. Referring to the border drawing, make border. You may have to adjust the border to fit your quilt top, in which case work from the corners towards the centre and adjust in the centre.

Using border fabric cut 2 strips 63½" x 1½" (1 613 mm x 38 mm). Sew to left and right hand sides of quilt. Cut 2 strips 45½" x 1½" (1 156 mm x 38 mm). Join 2 sashing squares to either end of each strip. Sew one row to top and one row to bottom of quilt. Quilt as desired.
Bind quilt.

Templates: Pages 72, 73

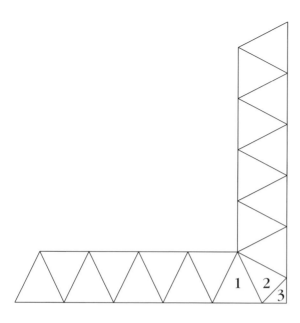

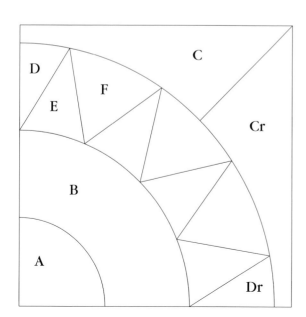

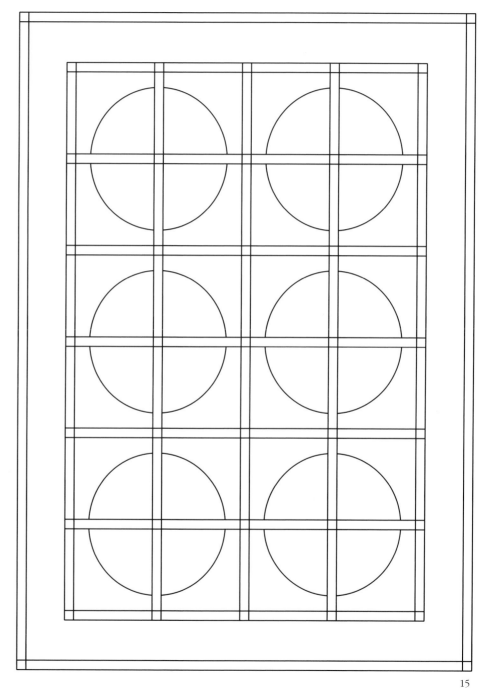

SCATTERINGS OF AFRICA

36" x 46"

91 cm x 117 cm

JENNY WILLIAMSON

The inspiration for this quilt was found in the African murals that are drawn by the artists freehand, therefore they are never accurately measured. This gives a naive character to their art, which is the look we wish to convey in this quilt. We have provided some applique shapes, but we suggest you choose a few of your own. Choose whatever shapes you find personify 'Africa', e.g. a particular tree, flower, animal, bird, etc. You would then applique the shapes you have chosen in rows across the background strips.

SCATTERINGS OF AFRICA

36" x 46"   91 cm x 117 cm

JENNY WILLIAMSON

This quilt can be made virtually any size. We suggest, however, that the width is not more than 43" **(110 cm)**, as it is more economical if the background and sashing strips are cut across the width of the fabric. Once you have decided upon the width of the quilt make as many background strips as are required to give the desired length.

Before starting this quilt please refer to the notes on machine applique.

TECHNIQUES:
Machine appliqued, machine pieced, machine quilted.
Applique and quilting can be done by hand if preferred.

MATERIALS:
The larger the variety of fabrics the better the quilt will look. Therefore you will need a variety of the following:

1) ¼ yd (¼ **m**) pieces suitable for backgrounds.
2) ¼ yd (¼ **m**) pieces suitable for the sashing strips and the applique.
Batting and backing 4" (10cm) larger both horizontally and vertically than the quilt top.
Binding.   ½ yd (½ **m**)
Iron-on vylene.   1 yd **(1 m)**

Applique and embroidery threads.

METHOD:
Cut your background strips in the following manner. Decide upon the horizontal measurement of your quilt. Cut your background strips this measurement by whatever widths are necessary for the shapes that you intend to applique.

Applique the shapes that you have chosen to the background strips.

Cut sashing strips the same measurement across as the background strips, but vary the vertical measurements.

Intersperse your sashing and background strips. Move them around until you are satisfied with the result.
Join all strips. (You may wish to insert a few narrow pleats and prairie points here and there to add interest).

Embellish the quilt with either machine or hand embroidery.
Frame your quilt with suitable fabric choosing a second fabric for the corner blocks. Quilt around the applique shapes and along some of the sashing strips to keep the work from stretching.
Bind quilt.

Templates: Page 71

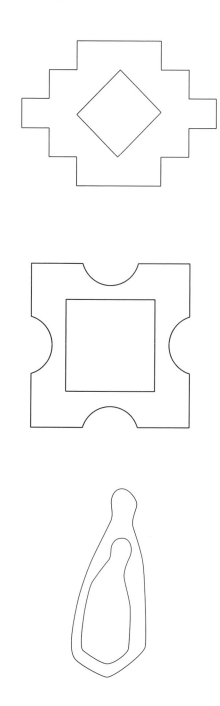

19

SIMUNYE VILLAGE

(Simunye *meaning* 'We Are One')

36" x 41"   91 cm x 104 cm

PAT PARKER AND JENNY WILLIAMSON

SIMUNYE VILLAGE

(Simunye *meaning* 'We Are One')

36" x 41"   91 cm x 104 cm

PAT PARKER AND JENNY WILLIAMSON

Before starting this quilt please refer to the notes on hand applique and choice of fabrics.

TECHNIQUES:
Hand appliqued, machine pieced, hand quilted.

MATERIALS:
To achieve a similar result as quilt featured in book you will require:

Background fabric (not too busy)	1 yd **(1m)**
Fabric suitable for huts	¼ yd **(¼ m)**

(The huts may either be worked in 1 or two pieces of fabric).
A variety of brightly coloured fabrics suitable for trees, people, borders, etc.

Batting.	40" x 45" **(102 cm x 115 cm)**
Backing.	40" x 45" **(102 cm x 115 cm)**
Binding.	½ yd **(½ m)**
Iron-on vylene.	1 yd **(1 m)**

Applique and embroidery threads.

METHOD:
Cut 1 piece of background fabric 20½" x 28½" **(520 mm x 724 mm)** (A).
Cut 3 pieces of background fabric 8½" x 10½" **(216 mm x 267 mm)** (B) (C) (D).
Applique these 4 pieces of fabric using the patterns provided.
Cut border strip 28½" x 2½" **(724 mm x 64 mm)** (E)
This may be one fabric or may be divided into blocks using a number of fabrics.
Sew to (A).
Cut (H) 22½ " x 6½" **(572 mm x 165 mm)**.
This may be one fabric or may be divided into a number of fabrics.

Add (H) to (A) and (E).
Cut 2 different fabrics 8½" x 2½" **(216 mm x 64 mm)** for (F) and (G). Join (B) (F) (C) (G) and (D) to (A) and (H).
Cut top border (J) 30½" x 3½" **(775 mm x 89 mm)**. Join to top of quilt.
Cut (K) 37½" x 3½" **(953 mm x 89 mm)** and join to left hand side of quilt.
Cut (L) 33½" x 4½" **(851 x 114 mm)** and join to base of quilt.
Cut (M) 41½" x 3½" **(1 054 mm x 89 mm)** and join to right hand side of quilt.
Embellish the quilt top with embroidery. Shadow quilt in rows on backgrounds approximately ¼" **(6 mm)** apart.
Bind quilt.

Templates: Pages 74, 75, 76

J

K

A

E

B

F

C

G

D

M

H

L

23

DARK SIDE OF THE MOON

44" x 54"   **112 cm x 137 cm**

JENNY WILLIAMSON

This is a Drunkard's Path quilt. It was made to show how one can take a basic traditional design and use 'African' fabrics.

Dark Side Of The Moon

44" x 54"   112 cm x 137 cm

JENNY WILLIAMSON

Before starting this quilt please refer to the notes on piecing and choice of fabrics.

TECHNIQUES:
Machine pieced and machine quilted.
This quilt may also be hand pieced and hand quilted.

BLOCK SIZE:
5" x 5" (127 mm x 127 mm) square. You will need 80 blocks.

MATERIALS:
This is a scrap quilt.
Introduce as many different fabrics into your blocks as possible.

Borders.   1 yd (1 m)
Backing.   48" x 58" (122 cm x 147 cm)
Batting.   48" x 58" (122 cm x 147 cm)
Binding.   ½ yd (½ m)

METHOD:
Cut templates exactly as they are on page 77, then add the ¼" (6 mm) seam allowance. Your piecing will be more accurate this way.
Using templates (A) and (B) cut 80 (A) and 80 (B). Join (A) to (B) along curve to form 80 blocks. Referring to diagram join blocks in rows - 6 blocks across by 8 blocks down.
Cut 2 strips 40½" x 1½" (1 029 mm x 38 mm) (C).
Add these strips to either side of quilt.
Referring to diagram, join 8 blocks and sew these to left hand side of quilt. Repeat for right hand side.

Cut 2 strips 42½" x 1½" (1 080 mm x 38 mm) (D).
Join these to top and bottom of quilt.
Cut 4 strips 5½" x 1½" (140 mm x 38 mm) (E).

Once again referring to diagram join top and bottom rows as follows:

1 block, 1 strip (E), 6 blocks, 1 strip (E) , 1 block. Add these 2 rows to top and bottom of quilt.
Cut 2 strips 52½" x 1½" (1 334 mm x 38 mm) (F). Join to either side of quilt.
Cut 2 strips 44½" x 1½" (1 130 x 38 mm) (G). Add to top and bottom of quilt.
Quilt as desired.
Add binding.

Templates: Page 77

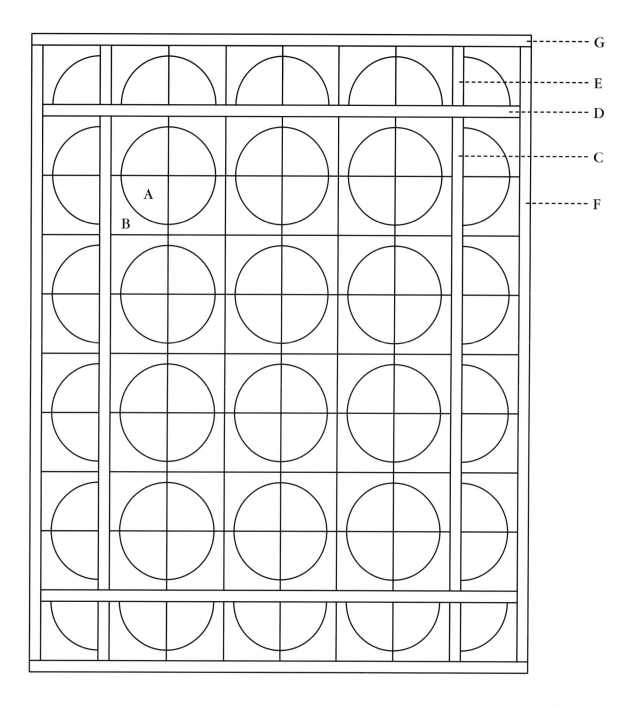

G

E

D

C

A

B

F

Road To
Umtata

52" x 38"
132 cm x 96 cm

PAT PARKER AND
JENNY WILLIAMSON

Road To Umtata

52" x 38"   132 cm x 96 cm

PAT PARKER AND JENNY WILLIAMSON

Before starting this quilt please refer to the notes on hand applique and choice of fabrics.

TECHNIQUES:
Hand appliqued, machine pieced and hand quilted.

BLOCK SIZE:
12" x 12"(305 mm x 305 mm) square. Make 6 blocks.

MATERIALS:

Background fabric.	1 yd (1 m)
Sashing strips.	1 yd (1m)
Sashing squares.	¼ yd (¼ m)
Inner border.	¼ yd (¼ m)
Outer border.	1½ yds (1½ m)
Backing.	56" x 42" (142 cm x 106 cm)
Batting.	56" x 42" (142 cm x 106 cm)
Binding.	½ yd (½ m)
Iron-on vylene.	1 yd (1 m)

Small scraps of brightly coloured fabrics suitable for applique.
Applique and embroidery threads.

METHOD:
Cut 6 background squares 12½" x 12½" (318 mm x 318 mm) (A).
Using the quilt photograph for reference applique 6 squares.
Cut 17 sashing strips 12½" x 2½" (318 mm x 64mm) (B) and
12 sashing squares 2½" x 2½" (64 mm x 64 mm).
Lay out the blocks 3 across by 2 down.
Working with the top 3 blocks add a sashing strip to the left side of each block and another strip to the right hand edge. Do the same with the second set of 3 blocks.

Sew 4 sashing squares to 3 sashing strips, alternating the squares and strips to form a row.
Make another 2 of these rows.
Sew these 5 rows together.

Using border fabrics
Cut 2 strips 30½" x 1½" (775 mm x 38 mm) (D)
Cut 2 strips 44½" x 1½" (1 130 mm x 38 mm) (E)
Cut 4 squares 1½" x 1½" (38 mm x 38 mm) (F)
Cut 2 strips 32½" x 3½" (826 mm x 89 mm) (G)
Cut 2 strips 46½" x 3½" (1 181 mm x 89 mm) (H)
Cut 4 squares 3½" x 3½" (89 mm x 89 mm) (J)
Sew strips (D) to left and right hand sides of quilt.
Join 2 squares (F) to either end of strips (E). Sew to top and bottom of quilt.
Sew strips (G) to left and right hand sides of quilt.
Join 2 squares (J) to either end of strips (H). Sew to top and bottom of quilt.
Embellish your quilt top with embroidery. Shadow quilt in rows on backgrounds approximately ¼" (6 mm) apart.
Bind quilt.

Templates: Pages 78, 79, 80, 81, 82

A

B

C

D

E

F

G

H

J

ELEPHANT HIDE

41" X 46"   **104 cm x 117 cm**

PAT PARKER

Elephants gather in family groups, but in spite of their size manage to 'hide' in the bush.

ELEPHANT HIDE

41" X 46"   104 cm x 117 cm

PAT PARKER

TECHNIQUES:

The geometric shapes on this quilt were machine appliqued and the elephants hand appliqued. This quilt may be made in either of these techniques, depending upon which of the two is preferred. Of course there are other motifs than elephants - the choice is up to the individual. The quilting may also be done by hand or machine.

MATERIALS:

Background fabric for strips.	1½ yds (1½ m)
8 to 10 fabrics suitable for applique.	1/8 yd each (1/8 m)
Fabric suitable for elephants (or motif of your choice)	¼ yd (¼ m)
Outer border and sashing strips	1¼ yd (1¼ m)
Inner border.	½ yd (½ m)
Backing.	45" x 50" (114 cm x 127 cm)
Batting.	45" x 50" (114 cm x 127 cm)
Binding.	½ yd (½ m)
Iron-on vylene.	1 yd (1 m)
Applique threads.	

METHOD:

Using background fabric cut 5 strips the following sizes:
1) 33½" x 7" (850 mm x 178 mm)
2) 33½" x 5½" (850 mm x 140 mm)
3) 33½" x 7" (850 mm x 178 mm)
4) 33½" x 11" (850 mm x 280 mm)
5) 33½" x 6" (850 mm x 152 mm)

Referring to quilt photograph, applique your geometric shapes onto the strips.
Cut 4 sashing strips 33½" x 1½" (850 mm x 38 mm).
Join 4 sashing strips to 5 background strips.
Using inner border fabric cut 2 strips 38½" x 1½" (978 mm x 38 mm) (A).

Add to left and right hand sides of quilt.
Cut 2 strips 35½" x 1½" (902 mm x 38 mm) (B) and add to top and bottom of quilt.
Using outer border fabric cut 2 strips 40½" x 3½" (1 029 mm x 89 mm) (C).
Add to left and right hand sides of quilt.
Cut 2 strips 35½" x 3½" (902 mm x 89 mm) (D)
Using a contrast fabric cut 4 squares 3½" x 3½" (89 mm x 89 mm) (E)
Join 1 square to each end of both strips.
Sew to top and bottom of quilt.
Applique the elephants (or motif of your choice) onto quilt top.
If using elephants they will need to be enlarged to required size.
Quilt around appliqued geometric shapes and motifs and also along sashing strips.
Bind quilt.

Drawings: Page 83
Templates: Pages 84 & 85

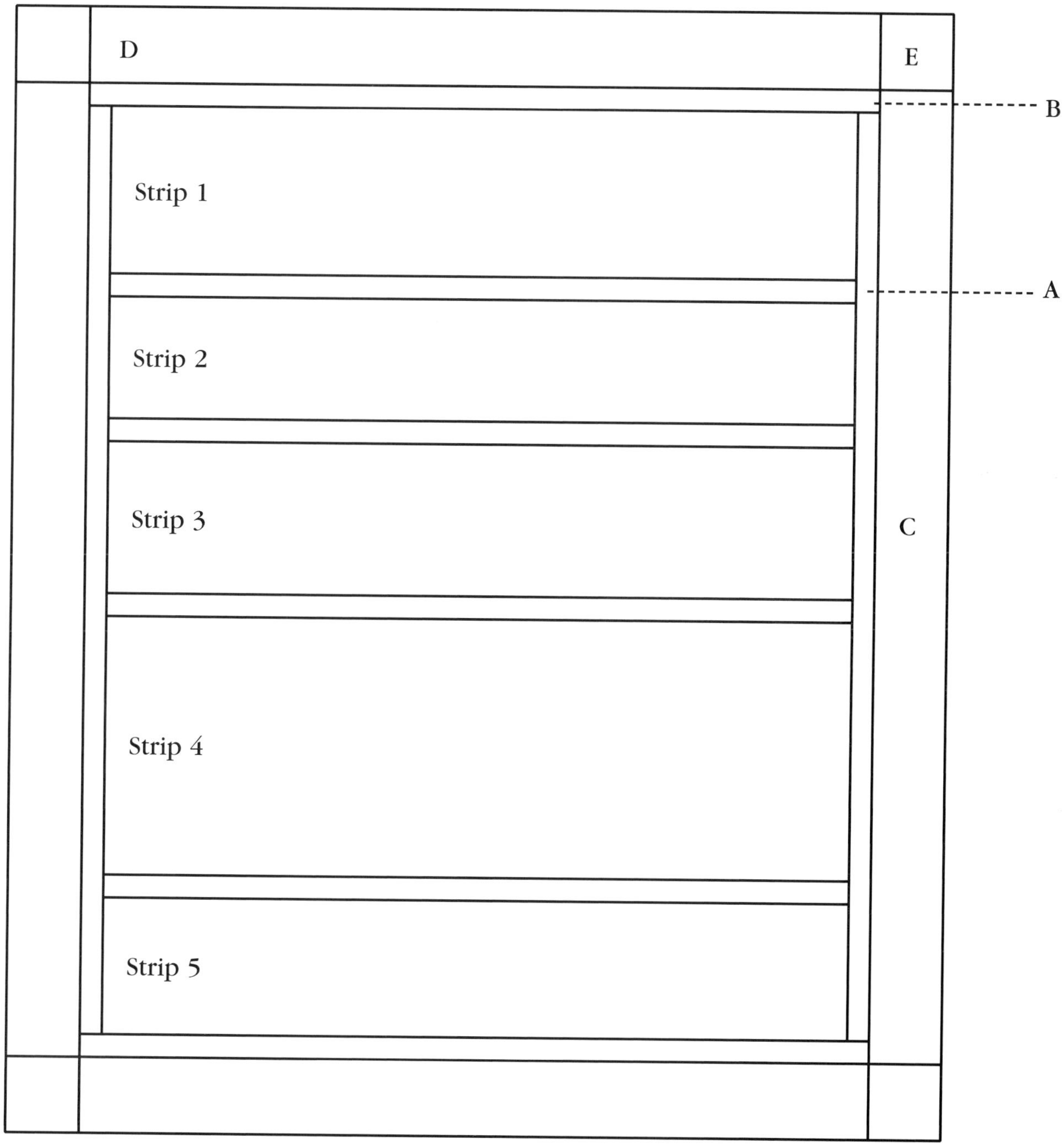

D

E

- - - - - - - - B

Strip 1

- - - - - - - - A

Strip 2

Strip 3

C

Strip 4

Strip 5

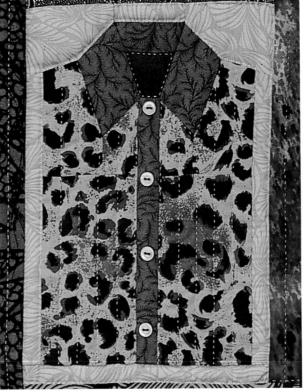

MANDELA LEADS THE WAY

44" X 56"   112 cm x 142 cm

PAT PARKER

MANDELA LEADS THE WAY

44" X 56"   112 cm x 142 cm

PAT PARKER

TECHNIQUES:
Hand pieced and hand quilted.

BLOCK SIZE:
7" x 10" **(178 mm x 254 mm)**. You will need 16 blocks.

MATERIALS:
16 Different fabrics suitable for shirts. (One piece of fabric approximately 9" x 12" **(228 mm x 305 mm)** will be sufficient for each shirt).
A variety of contrasting fabrics for shirt linings, collars, centre fronts and sashings between blocks.

Background fabric.	1 yd **(1 m)**
Border fabric.	½ yd **(½ m)**
Backing.	48" X 60" **(122 cm x 152 cm)**
Batting.	48" X 60" **(122 cm x 152 cm)**
Binding.	½ yd **(½ m)**
Shirt buttons.	64

As quilters don't as a rule 'do' buttons, perhaps the man in your life would oblige. Our husbands are far better at sewing on buttons than we are!

METHOD:
Make templates. See page 86
Mark your fabric, then add the ¼" **(6mm)** seam allowance.
Your piecing will be more accurate this way.
Please note that templates marked 'r' must be cut in reverse.
Cut 16 shirt blocks as follows:
Cut (A) (L) (Lr) (J) (Jr) and (K) from the background fabric.
Cut (B) (F) (Fr) and (D) from contrasting shirt fabrics.
Cut (C) from a fabric suitable for shirt lining.
Cut (E) (Er) (G) (Gr) (H) and (Hr) from shirt fabrics.

Step 1
Join background (A) to back collar (B) to shirt lining (C) to centre front (D).

Step 2
Join yoke (E) to collar (F) to yoke (G). Add on (H).

Step 3
Repeat Step 2 in reverse.

Step 4
Join units formed in Steps 1, 2 and 3.

Step 5
Add (J) and (Jr) to left and right hand sides of shirt. Join (K) to base of shirt and lastly add (L) and (Lr) to top left and right hand corners.

Step 6
Using a variety of contrasting fabrics cut 16 strips 7½" x 1½" **(191 mm x 38 mm)**. Add these to top of shirt.
Cut 16 strips 11½" x 1½" **(292 mm x 38 mm)**. Join to right hand side of shirt.
Cut 16 strips 8½" x 1½" **(216 mm x 38 mm)**. Join to base of shirt.
Cut 16 strips 12½" x 1½" **(318 mm x 38 mm)**. Join to left hand side of shirt.

Step 7
Join blocks in rows of 4 across by 4 down. Using main border fabric cut 2 strips 48½" x 4½" **(1 232 mm x 114 mm)** and add to left and right hand sides of quilt.
With the same fabric cut 2 strips 36½" x 4½" **(927 mm x 114 mm)**. Using a contrasting fabric suitable for corner blocks cut 4 squares 4½" x 4½" **(114 mm x 114 mm)**. Join 1 square to each end of both border strips. Sew to top and bottom of quilt.
Sew 4 buttons equally spaced down centre front of each shirt.
Quilt as desired.
Bind quilt.

Templates: page 86

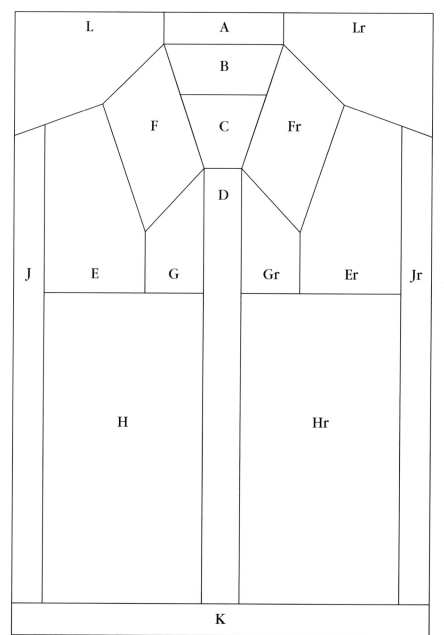

ESCAPES

45" X 40"   114 cm x 101 cm

JENNY WILLIAMSON

This quilt was inspired by a trip to Cape Town, hence the four scenes that are typical of this beautiful part of South Africa. However, using the same techniques as described below, any other landscapes may be chosen.

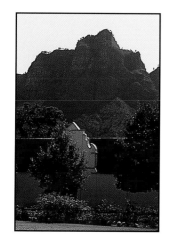

LEFT: ARNISTON

40" x 29"   1021 cm x 74 cm

JOAN INNES

Joan's quilt depicts a typical cape fishing cottage, with the fishermen discussing the catch of the day! Her choice of soft colours confirms the tranquility of the scene.

ESCAPES

45" X 40"   114 cm x 101 cm

JENNY WILLIAMSON

Fabric choice is the secret to successful scenic imagery. The sky sets the mood, e.g. it could be cloudy, sunny, misty, stormy, sunrise or sunset. The mountains may be steep and rugged, standing out clearly on the horizon, or they could be gentle pale slopes signifying distance. Water adds another mood. This could appear calm, flowing, deep, shallow, dark or glistening. The foreground may be lush pastures or sandy deserts. Decide on the mood of your picture and then depict this in fabric.

You may prefer to make a single picture (see Arniston on page 40 and Miracle of Namaqualand on page 50) or to make four pictures. Should you decide to make these four landscapes follow the instructions below. If not, exactly the same principle applies to any landscape picture.

Borders on landscapes are a personal choice and depend to a large extent upon the completed work. Choose your fabrics only when your landscape/s are complete. You may wish to add more applique to the borders. Either vine leaves, if following these instructions, or any other motif. (See Aloe Trail on page 56). Before starting this quilt please refer to our general notes on machine applique.

TECHNIQUES:
Machine applique and machine or hand quilting.

MATERIALS:
A variety of ¼ yd (¼ m) (fabrics suitable for skies, seas, mountains, etc.
Iron-on vylene.   1 yd (1 m)
Backing and Batting to be 4" (10 cm) larger than finished quilt size.
Binding.   ½ yd (¼ m)
Applique threads.

METHOD:
Drawings must be enlarged to desired size. Begin with the sky.
Trace off Piece No. 1 as marked adding an extra 1" (25 mm) seam allowance for top and each side of piece. Add on ¼" (6 mm) seam allowance to base.
Piece 2. Trace top as per drawing, add 1" (25 mm) to each side and ¼" (6 mm) to base.
Pieces 3 and 4. Same as piece 2.
Piece 5 (foreground). Add 1" (25 mm) to each side and 1" (25 mm) to base.
These extra seam allowances are added to allow you to square up your work after the landscape is complete.
Iron the vylene pieces to your fabrics. Cut exactly on the edge of the vylene. Tack the pieces in position.
Sew together.
Complete all 4 landscapes in this manner.
Square off landscapes.
Add borders as desired.
Applique motifs on borders.
Quilt as desired.
Bind quilt.

Drawings: Pages 87 & 88

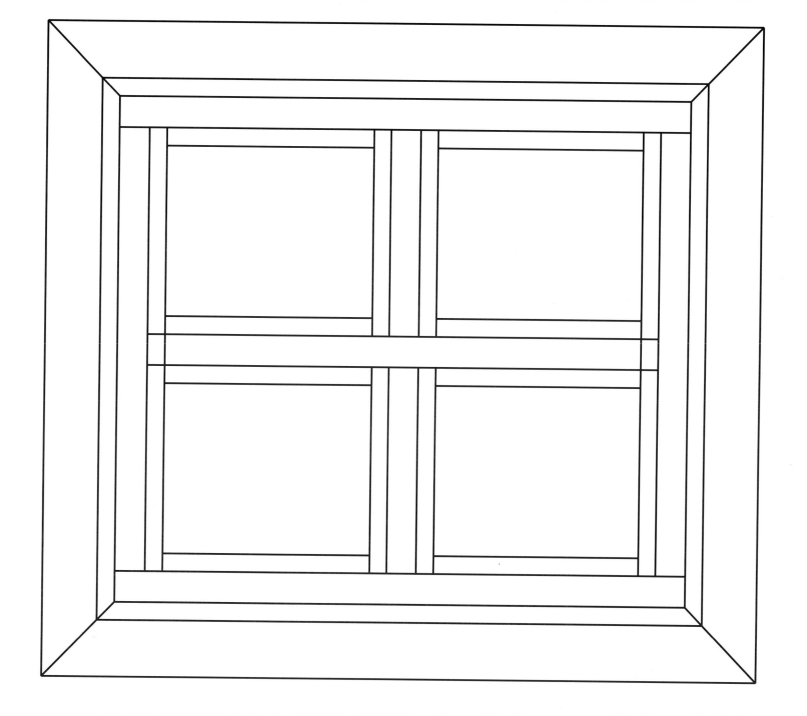

44

SUNBONNET SUE GOES ON SAFARI

56" x 68¹/₂"   **142 cm x 174 cm**

PAT PARKER AND JENNY WILLIAMSON

SUNBONNET SUE GOES ON SAFARI

56" x 68¹/₂"   142 cm x 174 cm

PAT PARKER AND JENNY WILLIAMSON

Before starting this quilt please refer to the notes on hand applique and choice of fabrics. Bear in mind when choosing the fabrics that hand-dyed fabrics work extremely well. Your backgrounds should be light to medium in value. Keep the strong colours for the foreground shapes.

TECHNIQUES:
Hand appliqued, machine pieced and hand quilted.

BLOCK SIZE:
The blocks should be 11" x 11" (**280 mm x 280 mm**) square (excluding seam allowance). Please enlarge the designs to this size.

MATERIALS:
Fabric to be used for the skies and
for the appliqued border.   2 yds (**2m**)
Fabric for hut roofs.   ¹/₄ yd (**¹/₄ m**)
Fabric for hut walls.   ¹/₄ yd (**¹/₄ m**)
A variety of fabrics suitable for the applique work.
Sashing strips between blocks and outside border.   2 yds (**2 m**)
Backing.   60" x 72" (**152 cm x 184 cm**)
Batting.   60" x 72" (**152 cm x 184 cm**)
Binding.   ¹/₂ yd (**¹/₂ m**)
Iron-on vylene.   2 yds (**2 m**)
Applique and embroidery threads.

METHOD:
Using the applique border background fabric cut the following pieces:

2 strips 51¹/₂" x 7" (**1 308 mm x 178 mm**) (D)
2 strips 39¹/₂" x 7" (**1 003 mm x 178 mm**) (E)
4 squares 7" x 7" (**178 mm x 178 mm**) (F)
Applique the 12 blocks, the 4 border strips and the 4 border squares.

Cut sashings as follows:
16 strips 11¹/₂" x 2" (**292 mm x 51 mm**) (B)
5 strips 39¹/₂" x 2" (**1 003 mm x 51 mm**) (C)
Lay out the blocks 3 across by 4 down.
Working with the top 3 blocks add a sashing strip to the left side of each block and another strip to the right hand edge.
Do the same with the other 3 rows of blocks. Join the 4 rows to the long sashing strips, one strip between each row and one at top and bottom. Sew the appliqued border strips (D) to the left and right hand sides of quilt.
Join 2 border squares (F) to the 2 appliqued strips (E).
Sew to top and bottom of quilt.
Cut 2 strips out of sashing fabric 64¹/₂" x 2¹/₂" (**1 638 mm x 64 mm**) (G)
Sew these 2 strips to the left and right hand side of quilt.
Cut 2 more strips out of sashing fabric 56¹/₂" x 2¹/₂" (**1 435 mm x 64 mm**) (H). Sew to top and bottom of quilt.
Embellish your quilt with embroidery.
Shadow quilt in rows ¹/₄" (**6 mm**) apart.
Bind quilt.

Drawings: Pages 92, 93, 94, 95
Templates: Page 96

H

E

F

C

A   B

D   G

47

AFRICAN DOLL

Thandi *meaning* Beloved.

8"   **20 cm**

PAT PARKER AND JENNY WILLIAMSON

TECHNIQUES:
Can be sewn either by hand or machine.

MATERIALS:
Brown cotton fabric suitable for body and feet. 14" x 7" **360 mm x 180mm**
Brightly coloured fabric suitable for dress and headdress.   ¼ yd (¼ **m**)
Small packet stuffing.
2 split key rings 1" **(25 mm)** in diameter (inside measurement)
2 split key rings 5/8" **(15 mm)** in diameter (inside measurement)
2 small rings suitable for earrings.
1 x 20" **(50 cm)** length strong black thread.
1 x 20" **(50 cm)** length red embroidery thread.
1 x 20" **(50 cm)** length white embroidery thread.

CUTTING:
Dress -   Cut 2
Body -   Cut 2
Feet -   Cut 4
Headdress -   Cut 1

METHOD:
Note: All seam allowances ¼" **(6 mm)**
If sewing by hand use small backstitch.

Body
Sew body leaving open at base. Clip corners, turn right side out. Stuff head firmly, place 2 large split key rings in position around neck, stuff arms and body firmly and stitch base closed.

Feet:
Sew feet, leaving top open. Trim seams, turn right side out, stuff lightly and stitch base closed.

Dress:
Turn under top of dress on foldline as indicated on pattern and press. With right sides facing sew the sides and base leaving open gaps for arms and feet.

Turn dress right side out and press lightly along the seams. Push feet through open gaps. Using small blind hemming stitches, stitch feet in position.

Starting at centre back and using strong black thread run a gathering stitch ¼" **(6 mm)** from the top edge of dress ending where you started. Slip body into dress extending arms through side openings. Pull up gathering thread and tie knot around neck. Trim ends of thread.

Headdress:
Turn in ¼" **(6 mm)** on straight edge of headdress and press. Fold around head as indicated on diagrams.
Stitch headdress to head along edge of headdress, sewing earrings in position as you go. Stitch top of headdress down as indicated on diagram.

Using 2 strands of embroidery thread embroider nose and eyes.
Use stem-stitch for nose and 3 French-knots for eyes.
Place bracelets on arms.

Templates: Pages 89, 90, 91

AFRICAN DOLL

Thandi *meaning* Beloved.

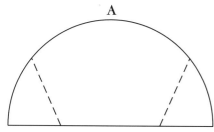

A

FOLD 1

B

FOLD 2

C

FOLD 3 AND 4

D

MIRACLE OF NAMAQUALAND

48" x 40"   **122 cm x 102 cm**

JENNY WILLIAMSON

Machine pieced, machine quilted.

In Spring, after a shower of rain, hundreds of varieties of seeds push their way up through the arid ground and stones, to produce a profusion of flowers - a miracle that makes its way into the soul of all who witness it. The total effect produced here is one of masses of flowers, a far distant horizon and a sky that goes on forever!

CHAPTER II

QUILTS TO BE INSPIRED BY

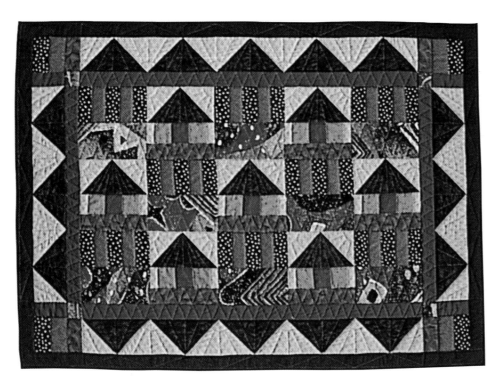

I KYALAMI (MY HOME)

50" x 36"   127 cm x 92 cm

PAT PARKER

Machine pieced, hand quilted.

This design is a repeat of a very basic block ; however, the use of vibrant colours ensures a striking impact.

OUT OF SEASON

42" x 32"   107 cm x 81 cm

GAYE BERTRAM

Machine appliqued, machine pieced, hand quilted.

This inspiration came from a greeting card by Claudette Barns. The guinea fowl is an incredibly decorative bird that roams around in the wild. With a little artistic licence a really bright, sunny effect was achieved.

STARLIGHT OVER AFRICA

40" x 50"   **102 cm x 127 cm**

PAT PARKER

Machine appliqued, machine pieced, hand quilted.

This is an innovative quilt using basic traditional techniques.
It is a 4-block design incorporating the 8-pointed star in the
borders.
The sashing strips are embellished with prairie points. The
hand-dyed fabrics used for the backgrounds of the blocks
enhance the feeling of infinite space.

MBASHE

32" x 32"   **81 cm x 81 cm**

JOY COWEN

After attending a one-day workshop Joy successfully depicted her personal observations of rural life. Her hand embroidery, beadwork, quilting and choice of border fabric all contributed to make this an enchanting piece of work.

AFRICAN AUTUMN

60" x 80"

152 cm x 224 cm

PAT PARKER

Machine pieced, hand quilted.

Inspired by the frequently quilt-like compositions of the geometric designs painted by rural African women on the walls of their homes. The warm, earthy colours suggest an autumnal feeling.

ALOE TRAIL

38" x 53"   96 cm x 135 cm

JOAN INNES

Machine appliqued, hand quilted.

Aloes are among South Africa's most attractive indigenous plants. This display of appealing colours is certain to attract the sunbirds!

RAPTORS

39" x 46"   **99 cm x 117 cm**

JOAN INNES

Machine appliqued, hand quilted.

The finer details of the birds of prey were hand embroidered.
Joan has a special empathy with a certain species of
endangered raptor (the Black Eagle) which circles the hills
near her home. The background fabric suggests the rocky
outcrops where the eagles nest.

MISTY MORNING IN HERMANUS

60" x 80"   **152 cm x 203 cm**

PAT PARKER

Machine pieced and hand quilted.

This quilt is a celebration of many happy days spent in Hermanus. The soft muted colours chosen are identical to those of the early morning mists that appear frequently in this beautiful area of South Africa.

Waterhole In The Moonlight

25" x 21"
65 cm x 55 cm
JOY COWEN

Machine appliqued.

Joy's wonderful reflections were created using layers of shiny organza and netting. Her choice of soft, muted colours suggests a tranquil atmosphere of silvery moonlight.

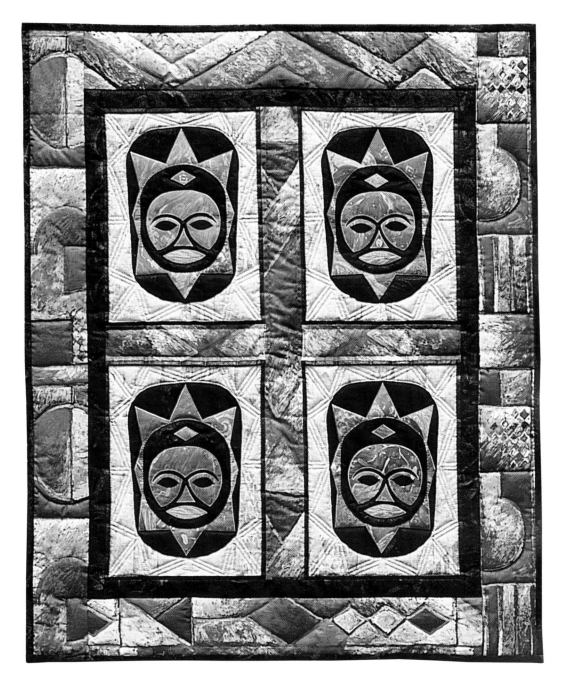

MASQUERADE

38" x 44"   96 cm x 112 cm

PAT PARKER AND JENNY WILLIAMSON

Machine appliqued, machine pieced, hand quilted.

In this quilt the contrast between the vivid colours and the black highlights the drama and mystery of these masks which play an important role in African culture.

SUNBURST

34" x 36"   **86 cm x 92 cm**

MARIE-CLAIRE STORME

Hand appliqued. Embellished by hand and machine.

Marie-Claire's choice of vibrant fabrics is dramatic. One can almost feel the heat of the sun radiating out of this quilt!

Ezulweni (A Piece Of Heaven)

42" x 54"   107 cm x 137 cm

LIBBY STEEL

Machine appliqued, machine pieced, hand quilted.

This quilt was made according to the instructions for *"Scatterings of Africa"* (see page 17.)
Libby's choice of fabrics and motifs produce an entirely different look and show her individual style. This is a good example of how to personalise a quilt and achieve a successful result.

QUIET BEFORE
THE STORM

45" x 39"   **114 cm x 99 cm**

PAT PERRY

Machine appliqued.
Hand quilted.

After the heat of the day a storm
threatens. The shadows
lengthen - a herd of buffaloes
make their way slowly to shelter
under the acacia trees. In this
quilt the atmosphere of the
African bushveld is so well
captured by the correct choice
of fabrics.

A VILLAGE IN AFRICA

44" x 54"

112 cm x 137 cm

PAT PARKER

Hand appliqued, hand quilted.
This is a simple portrayal of a traditional hut. The four-petalled form chosen for the background quilting frequently appears on African murals.

LINDIWE (WE ARE WAITING)

17½" x 23"

45 cm x 58 cm

BARBARA TUCKER

Machine appliqued, machine quilted.
In many areas of southern Africa women walk far with a bucket on their heads to obtain drinking water for their families. They wait patiently in the queue at the water-point chatting to their friends. The undulating hills in the background capture an illusion of endless space.

CHAPTER III

TEMPLATES AND DRAWINGS

Leap Year in the Lowveld

Drawings

Leap Year in the Lowveld

Drawings

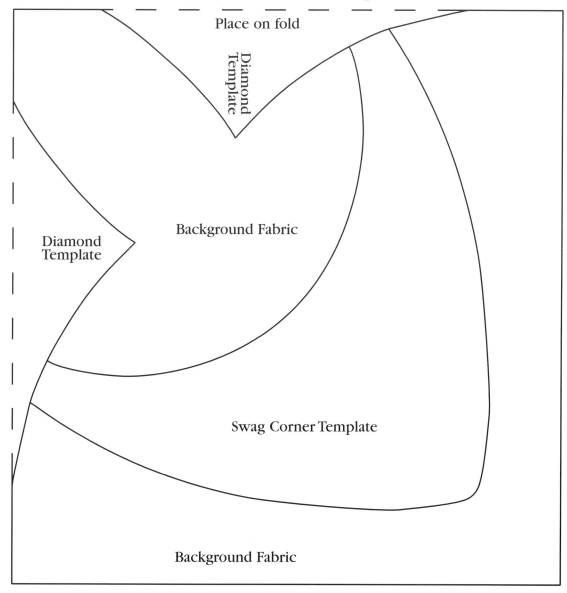

Applique Border Corner Templates

Place on fold

Diamond Template

Diamond Template

Background Fabric

Swag Corner Template

Background Fabric

Leap Year in the Lowveld

Template

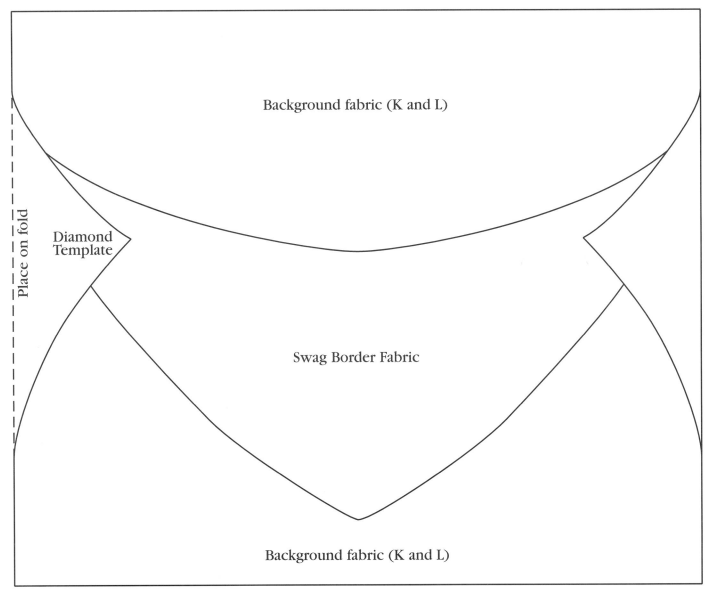

Background fabric (K and L)

Place on fold

Diamond
Template

Swag Border Fabric

Background fabric (K and L)

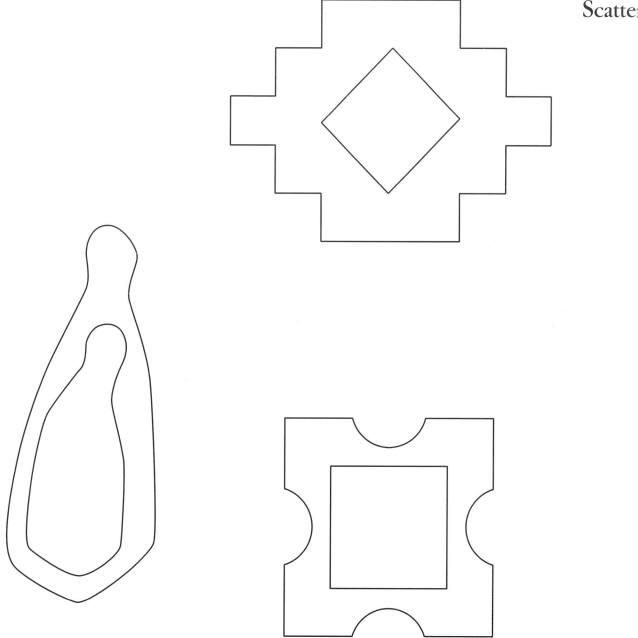

African Sunburst

Templates

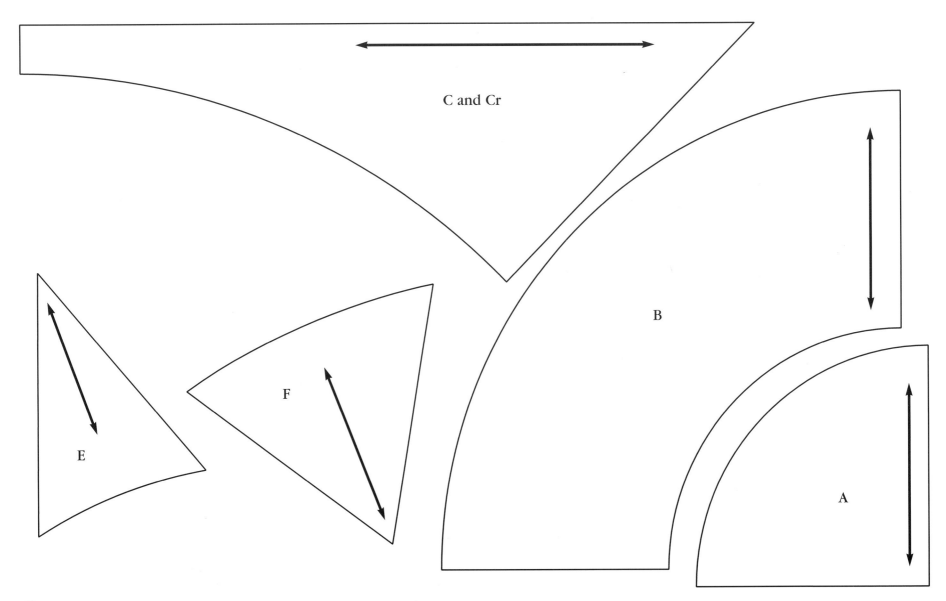

C and Cr

B

A

E

F

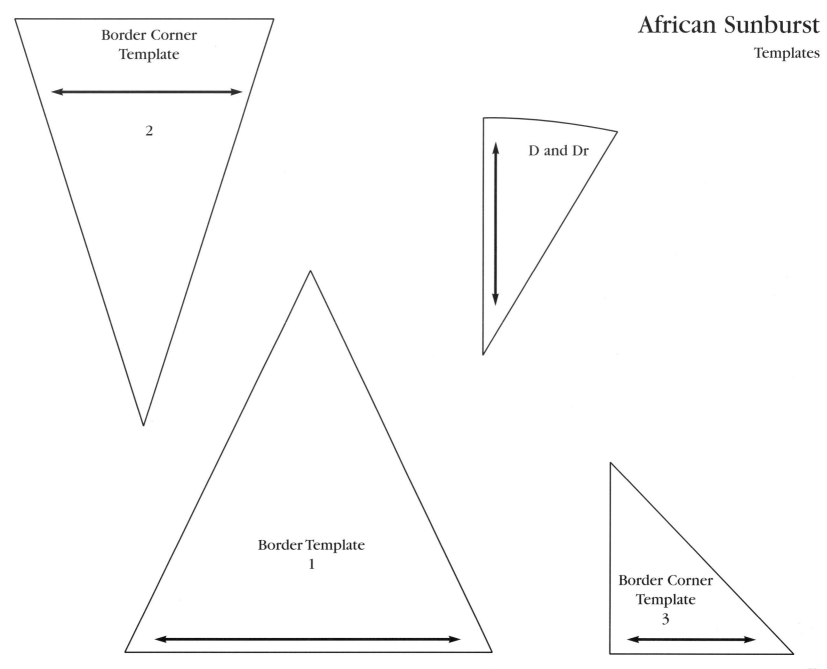

African Sunburst

Templates

Border Corner
Template

2

D and Dr

Border Template
1

Border Corner
Template
3

Simunye Village

Templates

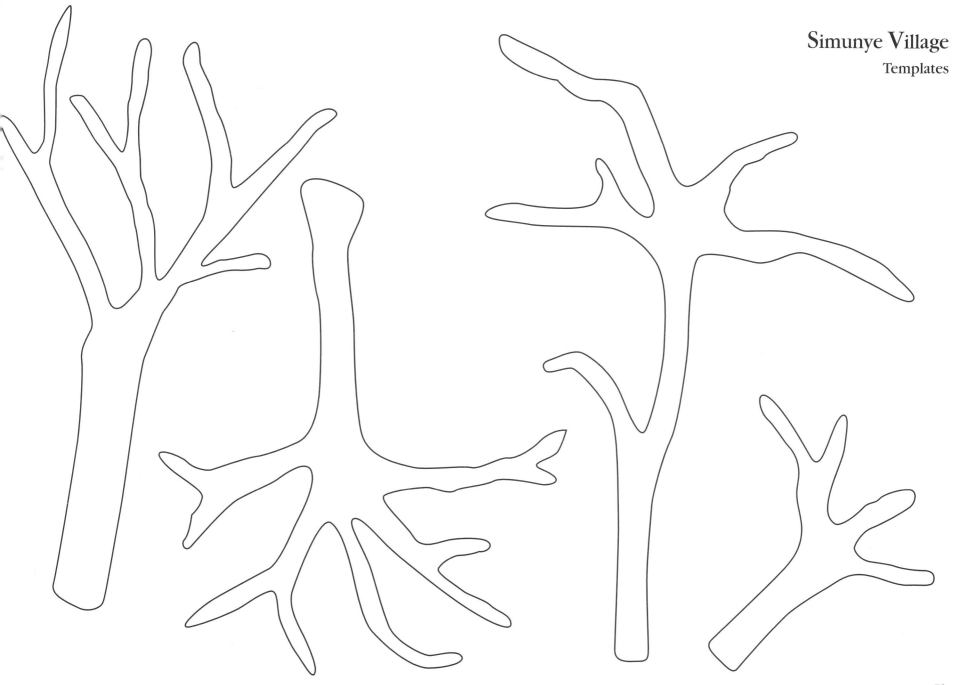

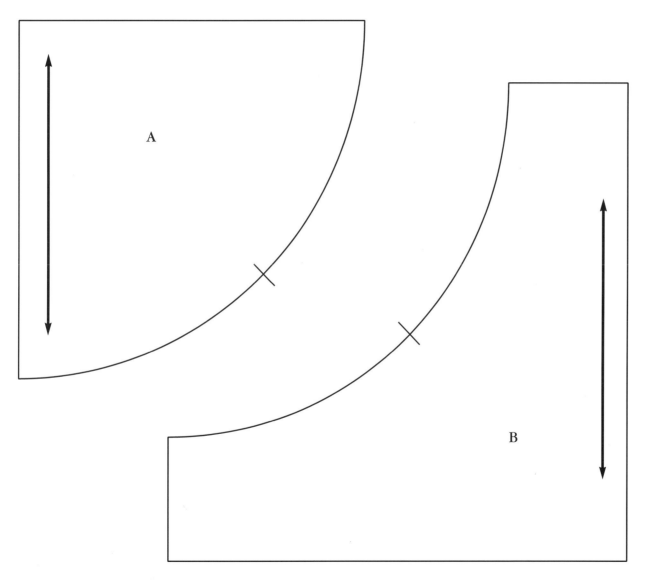

Road to Umtata

Templates

Road to Umtata

Templates

Road to Umtata

Templates

Elephant Hide

Templates

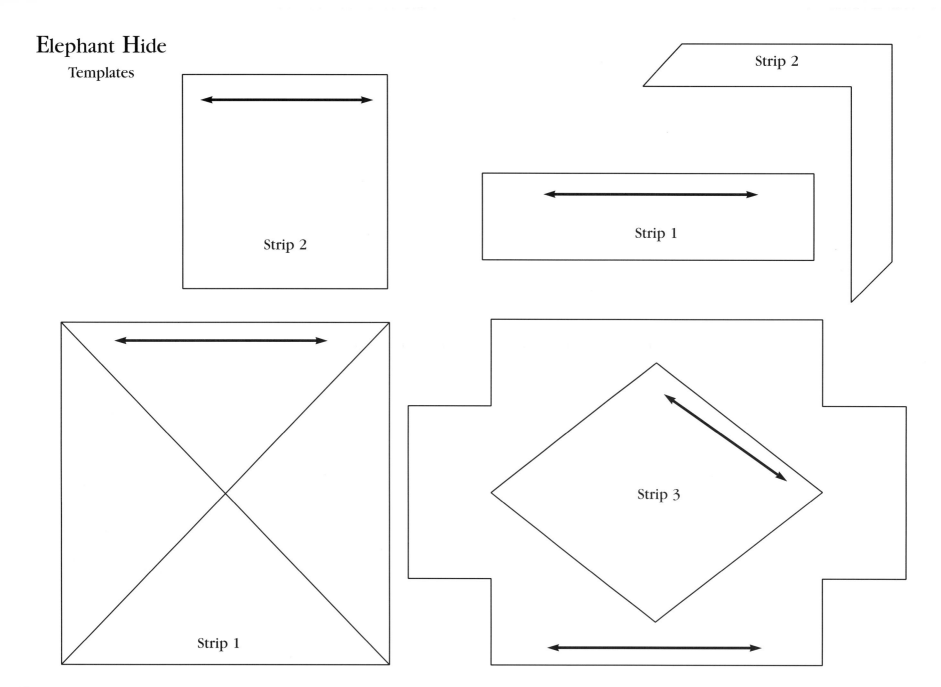

Strip 2

Strip 2

Strip 1

Strip 1

Strip 3

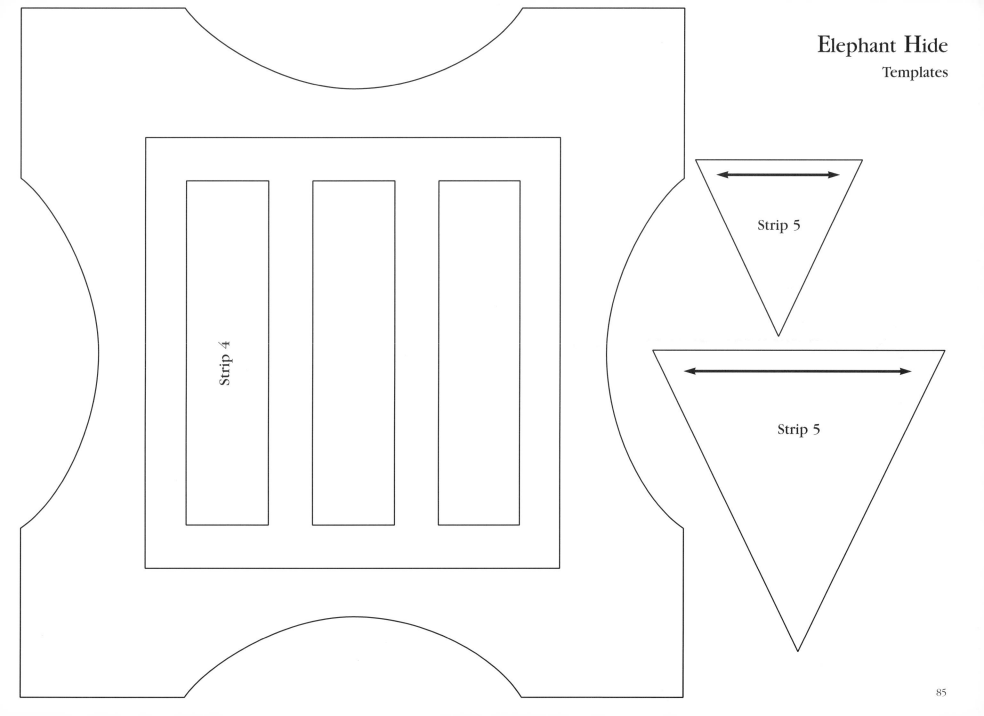

Elephant Hide

Templates

Strip 4

Strip 5

Strip 5

Mandela Leads the Way

Templates

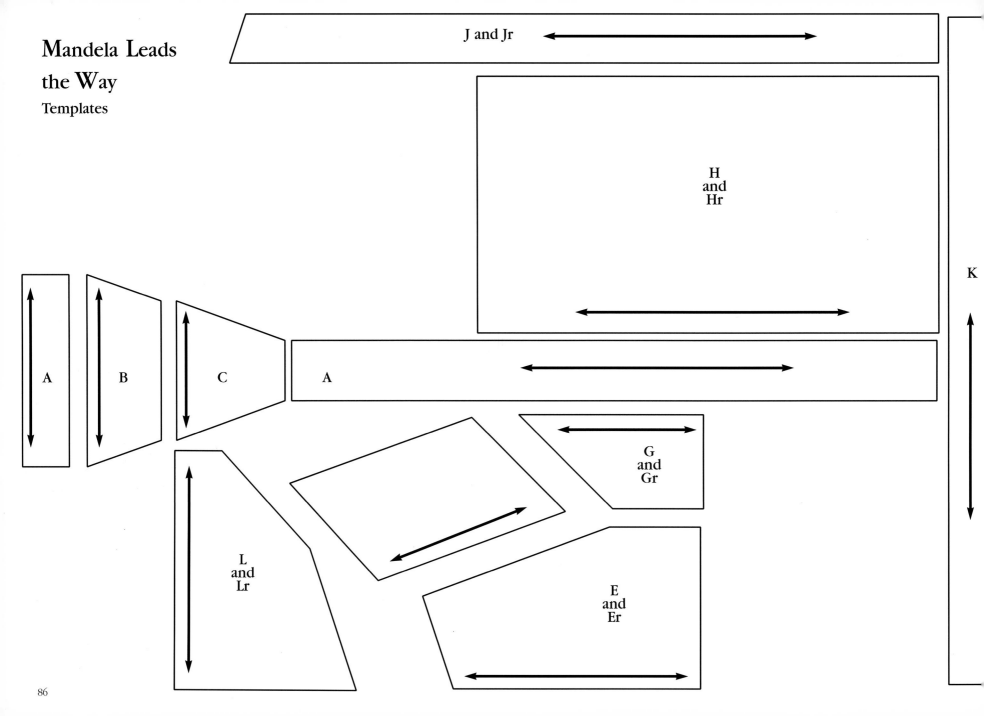

J and Jr

H
and
Hr

K

A

B

C

A

G
and
Gr

L
and
Lr

E
and
Er

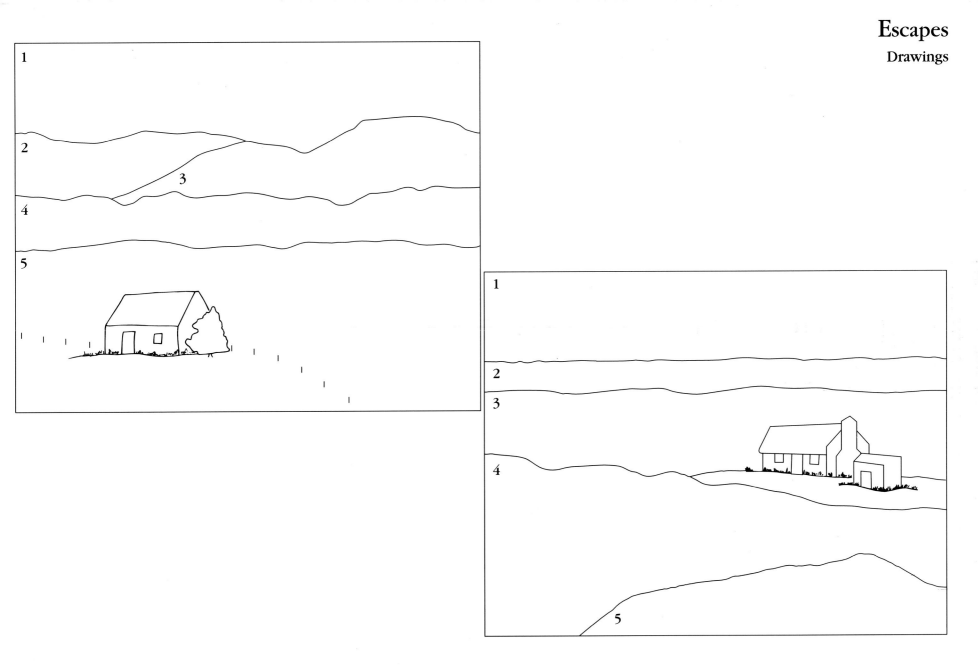

Escapes

Drawings

Body Cut 2

African Doll

Templates

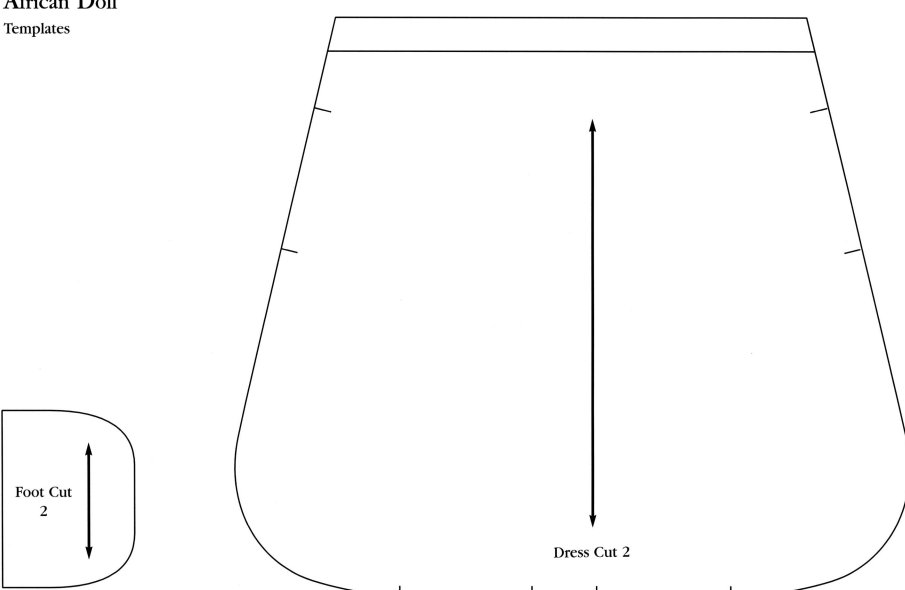

Foot Cut
2

Dress Cut 2

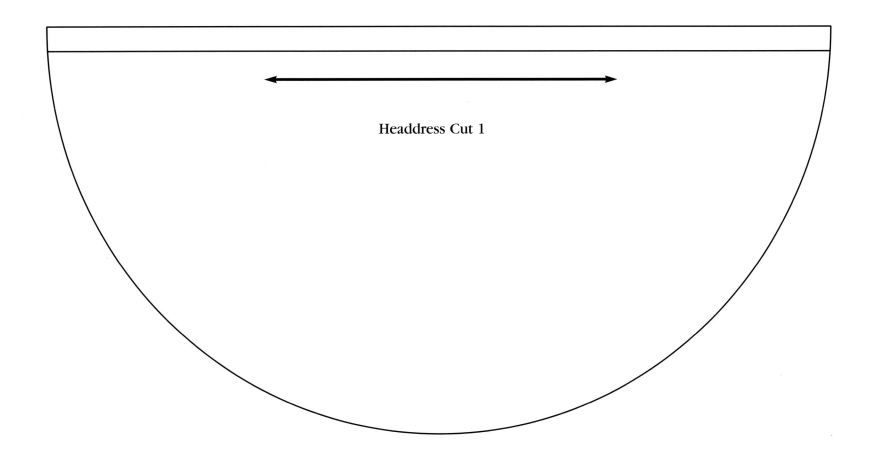

Headdress Cut 1

Sunbonnet Sue Goes on Safari

Drawings

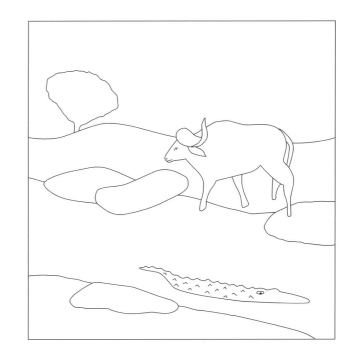

Sunbonnet Sue Goes on Safari

Drawings

Sunbonnet Sue Goes on Safari

Templates